PHOTOGRAPHY YEARBOOK 1993

INTERNATIONALES JAHRBUCH DER FOTOGRAFIE 1993

PHOTOGRAPHY YEARBOOK 1993

INTERNATIONALES JAHRBUCH DER FOTOGRAFIE 1993

edited by
PETER WILKINSON FRPS

Fountain Press

FOUNTAIN PRESS LIMITED

Queensborough House
2 Claremont Road
Surbiton
Surrey KT6 4QU
England

© FOUNTAIN PRESS 1992

Designed by Sally Stockwell

Reproduction and Printing by
Regent Publishing Services Ltd
Hong Kong

Deutsche Ausgabe:
© 1992 Wilhelm Knapp Verlag,
Niederlassung der Droste Verlag GmbH, Düsseldorf.
ISBN 3-87420-173-2

CONTENTS

INTRODUCTION

Change is rarely sudden. Often it is so subtle, so slowly evolving, that it can only be judged from a distance of many years and nowhere is this more true than in assessing the changes taking place in the art of photography. It is therefore interesting to note that the late Reggie Mason, Editor of *Photography Yearbook* ten years ago, remarked in his Introduction to the 1983 edition that it was impossible to identify underlying trends in photography in the space of only one year; over a decade, however, one was able to see clearly the changes that had taken place. He added his view that many monochrome photographs published or exhibited in 1973 would not have been acceptable ten years later, and that, equally, many pictures accepted in 1983 would have been immediately rejected ten years earlier.

This divergence of views is as much the effect of changes in fashions and attitudes as it is of developments to the technology of photography – time, again, is needed before any definition of such changes can be attempted. Plainly, successive Editors of *Photography Yearbook* will have had differing ideas about what should be included and what not, but even allowing for personal taste, a comparison of this edition with those from 1983 and 1973 shows clearly the changes that have taken place over two decades. It should be added, too, that before any changes in photographic trends can be considered, we must take into account marked improvements in the standard of book reproduction over these years, improvements which nowadays permit an altogether more faithful reproduction of the original monochrome or colour images.

Perhaps the most obvious change over the last twenty years is the enormous increase in the popularity of colour photography, largely because of the increasing ease and diminishing cost of producing colour prints. This, allied to the already-mentioned improvements in book-production techniques, is strongly reflected in the *Yearbook's* make-up, with its increasing numbers of colour pages: 48 in both 1973 and 1983, but 112 in this latest edition.

Visually, and as is only to be expected, there have been many changes in the type and style of photographs submitted and selected during this twenty-year period. In 1973, many of the images in the *Yearbook* relied on impact to make a strong, though not necessarily satisfying, impression; many of the portraits – often of 'personalities' of the day – were over-large and sombre; there were a number of 'news'-type photographs; natural history subjects were well below the standards to which, in 1992, we have become accustomed. Interestingly, comparing the Data Section shows that there is little difference in the cameras used twenty years ago and those favoured today, the main change being that zoom lenses – a fairly recent addition to the photographer's armoury – are now in much more widespread use.

The *Yearbook* for 1983 gives quite a different impression. Ten years on, it seems that the contributors were not taking life quite so seriously, for there is far more humour evident in their work. Some of the experimental works, however, seem over-contrived, and, again, the landscape and natural history photography lacks the feeling and quality of today's images. Although the 1983 edition has few 'news' photographs, there were a number of 'Royal' and 'famous-people' pictures, some of them humorous, while the unique style of Eastern European photographers – experts in making the ordinary appear interesting – made a strong contribution to the book.

Surprisingly, perhaps, none of the photographers from the 1973 *Yearbook*, and only two from 1983, are represented in this year's edition. I would also estimate that less than a quarter of the pictures from the 1973 edition, and less than half from 1983, would be considered suitable for inclusion today. Obviously, technical improvements (as well as, though to a lesser extent, fashion and personal taste) account for this in part, but a strong contributing factor must be the huge increase in recent years in the number of good pictures submitted, so that the Editor has far greater scope for his selection than did his predecessors.

Photography Yearbook's international flavour has also been greatly enhanced over the last two decades, the number of countries represented rising from twenty-one in 1973 to thirty-two in this year's edition. Far-reaching political upheavals in Europe and economic recession throughout the world, seem to have had little or no effect upon the desire of contemporary photographers to see their work published in the 1993 *Yearbook* – we have seen more pictures, and of greater quality overall, submitted this year than ever before. Perhaps, then, that is the greatest change that these past twenty years have wrought – more and better photographs submitted, and more and better photographs chosen and printed. And that can only be a change for the better.

PETER WILKINSON, FRPS
Editor, August 1992

The closing date for receiving material at the publishers for possible inclusion in the next edition of Photography Yearbook *is the end of January 1993 and this will apply to subsequent years.*

Colour transparencies may be of any size but should not be glass mounted. If a colour picture is available both as a print and as a transparency, the transparency is preferred. Prints, both black and white and colour, should be unmounted and not smaller than 18 x 24cm or larger than 30 x 40cm. Prints should always be packed flat not rolled. All work submitted must carry the author's name, and information is required as to the location or subject and any points of interest relating to the picture as well as to the make of camera, lens and film used.

If packing is suitable, and adequate return postage in Sterling cheques, money orders or twelve International Reply Coupons is included, work will be returned after the book has been finalised. Non-United Kingdom entries will be returned by surface mail unless sufficient additional remittance is included to cover airmail.

All possible care will be taken by Fountain Press, but they cannot be held responsible for any loss or damage that might occur to material submitted. Although the copyright of any work accepted remains with the author, the publisher may use accepted pictures to publicise Photography Yearbook.

As well as the prestige of having their work published, successful contributors will receive a copy of Photography Yearbook *and a reproduction fee. Upon request, the Publisher will, where possible, put prospective picture buyers in touch with the authors of successful pictures.*

EINFÜHRUNG

Eine Veränderung tritt selten unvorhergesehen ein. Oftmals ist sie so unmerklich, entwickelt sich so langsam, daß man sie nur aus einer Distanz von mehreren Jahren beurteilen kann; und nirgends trifft dies mehr zu, als in der Kunst der Fotografie. Daher ist es interessant, daß Reggie Mason, Herausgeber des *Photography Yearbook* vor zehn Jahren, in seiner Einleitung zur Ausgabe 1983 bemerkte, daß es unmöglich sei, zugrundeliegende Trends in der Fotografie in einem Zeitraum von einem Jahr nachzuweisen; nach einem Jahrzehnt könne man erst deutlich die stattgefundenen Veränderungen erkennen. Er fügte dem noch hinzu, daß viele einfarbige Fotos, die 1973 veröffentlicht und ausgestellt wurden, zehn Jahre später nicht akzeptiert würden und ebenso viele Bilder, die 1983 akzeptiert wurden, zehn Jahre vorher sofort abgelehnt worden wären.

Diese Abweichung der Ansichten ist sowohl die Wirkung der Veränderungen in Mode und Verhalten, als auch die Entwicklung in der Technologie der Fotografie. Zeit wiederum ist nötig bevor man diese Veränderungen definieren kann. Erfolgreiche Herausgeber des *Photography Yearbook* sind unterschiedlicher Ansicht darüber, was veröffentlicht werden soll und was nicht, aber gerade diese persönliche Entscheidung in dieser Ausgabe im Vergleich zu denen von 1983 und 1973 zeigt deutlich die stattgefundenen Veränderungen aus zwei Jahrzehnten. Es sollte noch hinzugefügt werden, dass bevor man Veränderungen in fotografischen Trends beachten kann, die deutlichen Verbesserungen in der Art der Buchreproduktion berücksichtigt werden sollte; Verbesserungen, die heutzutage eine getreuere Reproduktion der original einfarbigen oder farbigen Bilder gestatten.

Vielleicht die deutlichste Veränderung in den letzten zwanzig Jahren ist der enorme Zuwachs in der Popularität der Farbfotografie, zum großen Teil aufgrund des verminderten Preises für die Produktion von Farbdrucken. Dieses, verbunden mit den bereits erwähnten Verbesserungen in der Technik der Buchproduktion, spiegelt sich deutlich in der Aufmachung des *Yearbook* wider; dieses zeigt die anwachsende Zahl von farbigen Seiten: 48 in den Ausgaben 1983 und 1973, aber 112 in dieser neuen Ausgabe.

Viele Veränderungen haben sich auch im Typus und Stil der Fotos ergeben, die während dieser zwanzigjährigen Periode ausgewählt wurden. Noch 1973 machten viele der Bilder im *Yearbook* einen starken, wenn auch nicht befriedigenden Eindruck. Viele Portraits, oftmals von Persönlichkeiten des aktuellen Geschehens, waren übergroß und düster, ferner gab es eine Anzahl von 'news'-type Fotos; natürliche historische Objekte lagen unter dem Standard, an den wir 1992 gewöhnt sind. Interessanterweise ergibt sich, wenn man die 'Data Sections' vergleicht, kaum ein Unterschied zwischen den Kameras, die vor zwanzig Jahren benutzt wurden und den heute bevorzugten: Die Zoom-Linsen, ein moderner Zusatz in der Ausrüstung des Fotografen, die heute weit verbreitet sind.

Das *Yearbook* 1983 macht einen ganz anderen Eindruck. Zehn Jahre später, so scheint es, nehmen die Mitarbeiter das Leben nicht mehr so schwer, offenbar haben sie mehr Humor bei ihrer Arbeit. Einige der experimentellen Arbeiten scheinen fiktiv und wiederum fehlt der landschaftlichen und historischen Fotografie das Gefühl und die Qualität heutiger Bilder. Obwohl in der Ausgabe von 1983 ein paar 'news' Fotos vorhanden waren, gab es mehrere Bilder königlicher und berühmter Leute, einige sehr humorvoll, während der einheitliche Stil osteuropäischer Fotografen, Experten die gewöhnliche Erscheinungen interessant machen, einen starken Beitrag zu dem Buch lieferten.

Überraschenderweise ist keiner der Fotografen des *Yearbooks* von 1973 und nur zwei aus 1983 in der diesjährigen Ausgabe vertreten. Ferner würde ich schätzen, daß weniger als ein Viertel der Bilder der Ausgabe 1973 und weniger als die Hälfte der Bilder der Ausgabe 1983 für die heutige Ausgabe in Frage kämen.

Offensichtlich liegt dieses zum Teil an den technischen Verbesserungen (und, wenn auch in geringem Ausmaße an Mode und persönlichem Geschmack), ein wichtiger Faktor ist jedoch auch der starke Zuwachs von guten Bildern in den letzten Jahren, so dass der Herausgeber einen größeren Spielraum bei seiner Auswahl hat, als seine Vorgänger.

Der internationale Geschmack des *Photography Yearbook* hat sich in den letzten zwei Jahrzehnten erhöht; die Anzahl der vertretenen Länder betrug 1973 einundzwanzig, in der diesjährigen Ausgabe sind es zweiunddreißig. Weitreichende politische Umwälzungen in Europa und wirtschaftliche Rückgänge in der ganzen Welt scheinen keine oder nur eine geringe Auswirkung auf zeitgenössische Fotografen zu haben, die nur den Wunsch hegen, ihre Arbeit im *Yearbook* 1993 veröffentlich zu sehen. Wir haben mehr Fotos von höherer Qualität in diesem Jahr gesehen, als in all den anderen Jahren.

Vielleicht ist dies die deutlichste Veränderung, die die letzten zwanzig Jahre hervorbrachte. Mehr und bessere Fotos wurden vorgelegt und mehr und bessere Fotos wurden ausgewählt und gedruckt.

Und dieses kann nur eine Veränderung zum Besseren hin sein.

PETER WILKINSON FRPS
Herausgeber, August 1992

Einsendeschluß für Material, das möglicherweise in der nächsten Ausgabe des Internationalen Jahrbuchs der Fotografie veröffentlicht wird, ist Ende Januar 1993. Zu diesem Zeitpunkt muß das Material beim Verleger eingelangt sein. Farbtransparente können von jeglicher Größe sein, dürfen jedoch nicht in Glasrahmen gesandt werden. Sollte ein Farbbild als Abzug und als Farbtransparent vorhanden sein, bitten wir um Einsendung des Dias. Alle Fotos — sowohl Schwarz/Weiß als auch Farb — sollen nicht aufgezogen, nicht kleiner als 18 x 24cm und nicht größer als 30 x 40cm sein. Abzüge sollen immer flach verpackt und nicht gerollt werden. Alle eingesandten Arbeiten müssen den Namen des Fotografen tragen, sowie Informationen über Aufnahmeort, spezielle Interessensfaktoren in Bezug auf die Aufnahme und vor allem Angaben über die verwendete Kamera, Linse und Film enthalten.

Wenn das Verspackungsmaterial entspricht und ausreichendes Retourporto in Form von Schecks in Englischen Pfunden oder Internationalen Antwortscheinen beigelegt ist, werden Arbeiten nach Verlagsabschluß des Buches retourniert. Fountain Press wird selbstverständlich alle arbeiten mit größter Sorgfalt behandeln, kann jedoch keinerlei Haftung für eventuelle Beschädigung oder Verluste des eingesandten Materials übernehmen. Wenn auch das Urheberrect der eingesandten Arbeiten dem Einsender zusteht, darf der Verleger angenommene Arbeiten im Internationalen Jahrbuch der Fotografie veröffentlichen.

Abgesehen vom Prestige ihre Arbeiten veröffentlicht zu sehen, werden erfolgreiche Teilnehmer auch eine Ausgabe des Internationalen Jahrbuchs der Fotografie und eine Reproduktionsgebühr erhalten. Auf Anfrage wird sich der Verlag bemühen, zukünftige Fotokäufer und Schöpfer erfolgreicher Bilder zusammenzuführen.

Wir hoffen, daß Sie am Internationalen Jahrbuch der Fotografie 1993 Freude haben und auch in Zukunft Ihre Arbeiten für mögliche Publikation in der nächsten Ausgabe einsenden werden. Fotos von Fotografen außerhalb Großbritanniens sind uns besonders willkommen, da diese helfen, den Internationalen Charakter dieses Buches aufrechtzuerhalten.

INTRODUCTION

Les changements sont rarement soudains. Ils sont souvent si subtils, si lents que l'on ne peut en juger qu'après de nombreuses années; et ceci n'est nulle part plus vrai que lorsqu'on veut évaluer les changements survenus dans l'art de la photographie. Aussi est-il intéressant de remarquerque feu Reggie Mason, éditeur du *Photography Yearbook* il y a dix ans, indiquait dans son Introduction au numéro de 1983 qu'il était impossible de préciser les tendances directrices de la photographie dans l'espace d'une seule année; dans l'espace d'une décennie cependant, il est possible de voir clairement les changements apparus. Il ajoutait, comme son opinion personnelle, que nombre des photographies monochromes, publiées ou exposées en 1973, n'auraient pas été acceptables dix ans plus tard; et que, de même, nombre des images acceptées en 1983 auraient été immédiatement rejetées dix ans plus tôt.

Cette divergence de vues tient autant aux changements de modes et d'attitudes qu'aux progrès de la technique photographique; et, une fois encore, il faut laisser passer un certain temps avant qu'il soit possible de les définir. Il est évident que les éditeurs successifs du *Photography Yearbook* auront des opinions variées sur ce qui doit être inclus et ce qui doit être refusé, mais même en tenant compte des différences de goûts individuels, la comparaison entre ce numéro et ceux de 1983 et de 1973 montre clairement les changements survenus au cours de ces deux décennies. Il faut dire aussi qu'avant de pouvoir considérer les changements des tendances de l'art photographique, on doit faire la part des progrès réalisés au cours de ces années dans la qualité de la reproduction, de nos jours beaucoup plus fidèle, des images monochromes et en couleurs.

Peut-être le changement le plus évident survenu au cours de ces vingt dernières années est-il le très grand développement de la popularité de la photographie en couleurs, dû surtout aux facilités accrues et à la diminution des frais de production des épreuves en couleurs. Ceci, ajouté aux progrès déjà mentionnés dans les techniques de reproduction, apparaît clairement dans la composition du *Yearbook*, le nombre des pages de photographies en couleurs étant de 112 dans la dernière édition, contre 48 en 1983 et en 1973.

Au point de vue visuel, comme on pouvait s'y attendre, de nombreux changements sont survenus dans le genre et le style des photographies proposées, et publiées, durant ces vingt dernières années. En 1973, beaucoup des images reproduites dans le *Photography Yearbook* avaient été choisies à cause d'une première impression très forte, mais n'etaient pas toujours d'une qualité satisfaisante; il y avait beaucoup de portraits de 'personnalités' du jour, très agrandis et sombres; également, un grand nombre de 'photos d'actualités'; et les sujets pris dans la nature étaient loin de la qualité à laquelle nous sommes accoutumés en 1992. Il est intéressant, en comparant les indications données par les sections consacrées aux informations techniques, de constater qu'il y a peu de différences entre les appareils utilisés il y a vingt ans et ceux utilisés aujourd'hui – la principale différence étant que les lentilles Zoom – un relativement récente addition à l'équipement photographique – sont maintenant d'un usage plus répandu.

Le *Yearbook* de 1983 donne une impression très différente. Il semble qu'en ces dix années, les contributeurs aient cessé de prendre la vie tellement au sérieux, leurs photographies révélant un beaucoup plus grand sens de l'humour. Certains des travaux de caractère expérimental semblent cependant un peu forcés; et, une fois encore, les paysages et les aspects de la nature n'offrent pas la qualité et la sensibilité que nous trouvons aux images d'aujourd'hui. Bien que l'édition de 1983 contînt peu de photos d' 'actualités', elle comportait un certain nombre de portraits de membres de la famille royale, et de 'célébrités', dont quelques-uns traités avec humour, tandis que le style unique des photographes des pays d'Europe de l'Est, particulièrement habiles à révéler l'aspect intéressant des choses de la vie ordinaire, apportait au livre une importante contribution.

Il est surprenant qu'aucun des photographes du *Yearbook* de 1973 – et deux seulement de celui de 1983 – ne soit représenté dans cette édition. Je crois pouvoir dire aussi que moins d'un quart des images publiées dans celle de 1973, et moins de la moitié dans celle de 1983, auraient pu être considérées comme acceptables dans celle de cette année. Il est certain que les progrès de la technique (et, bien qu'a un moindre degré, la mode et les goûts personnels) y sont pour beaucoup, mais il y a un autre facteur très important, que est l'énorme accroissement du nombre de bonnes photographies proposées, de sorte que l'éditeur s'est trouvé avoir un bien plus large choix que ses prédécesseurs.

Le caractère international du *Photography Yearbook* s'est également beaucoup développé au cours de ces deux décennies, le nombre des pays représentés étant passé de vingt-et-un en 1973 à trente-deux pour l'édition de cette année. Les événements de grande portée qui ont eu lieu en Europe, et par ailleurs la récession économique qui sévit dans le monde entier, ne semblent avoir eu que très peu de répercussions – sinon aucune – sur le désir qu'ont les photographes contemporains de voir leurs travaux publiés dans le *Yearbook* de 1993, et nous avons reçu cette année plus de photographies, et des photographies de meilleure qualité, que jamais encore. Il se peut, alors, que le plus grand changement que nous aient apporté ces vingt dernières années soit le plus grand nombre et la meilleure qualité des photographies proposées, et le plus grand nombre de meilleures photographies choisies et publiées. Et ceci ne peut être qu'un changement pour le meilleur.

PETER WILKINSON, FRPS
Editeur, août 1992

La date limite pour la réception des travaux soumis en veu d'une eventuelle publication dans le Photography Yearbook est le 31 janvier 1993, et ceci s'applique, mutatis mutandis, aux années suivantes. Les diapositives en couleurs peuvent être de n'importent quelles dimensions, mais ne doivent pas être montées sur verre. Au cas où une photographie en couleurs existe à la fois en épreuve et en diapositive, la diapositive sera préférée. Les épreuves, en blanc et noir ou en couleurs, ne doivent pas être montées, et ne doivent pas mesurer moins de 18 x 24cm, ni plus de 30 x 40cm. Les épreuves doivent toujours être emballées à plat, non roulées. Tous les travaux proposés doivent porter le nom de leur auteur, et l'indication du lieu, et d'autres faits relatifs à l'image, à l'appareil, à l'objectif et à la pellicule utilisés.

Si l'emballage est convenable, et l'envoi accompagné des frais de port sous forme de chèque ou de mandat sterling, ou de douze Coupons Réponse Internationaux, les travaux seront réexpédiés à leurs auteurs une fois achevée la préparation du livre. Les travaux reçus de pays autres que le Royaume-Uni seront renvoyés par courrier ordinaire à moins qu'ils ne soient accompagnés d'une somme suffisante à couvrir les frais de courrier par avion.

Bien que tous les envois soient traités avec le plus grand soin, Fountain Press ne peut accepter la responsabilité d'aucune perte ou dommage survenus au matériel reçu. Et bien que le copyright de toutes les photographies soit conservé par l'auteur, les éditeurs se réservent le droit de les utiliser à des fins de publicité pour le Photography Yearbook. Les contributeurs dont les travaux sont reproduits non seulement jouiront du prestige que leur confère la publication dans le Photography Yearbook, mais aussi recevront un exemplaire du livre et un droit de reproduction. Sur requête, la direction de Fountain Press pourra se charger, là où il sera possible, de mettre en relation les éventuels acheteurs avec les auteurs des photographies publiées.

INTRODUCCION

Un cambio rara vez sucede de repente. Suele ser algo sutil, de lenta evolución, que sólo puede juzgarse retrospectivamente tras muchos años. Ciertamente esto es lo que ocurre a la hora de juzgar los cambios que han tenido lugar en el arte de la fotografía. Es pues interesante notar que el fallecido Reggie Mason, autor de la edición del *Photography Yearbook* de hace diez años, comentó en su introducción a la edición de 1983 que es imposible identificar las corrientes fotográficas en el plazo de un año; sólo a lo largo de una década es posible ver los cambios que han tenido lugar. En su opinión, muchas de las fotografías monocromas publicadas o mostradas en 1973 hubieran sido inaceptables diez años más tarde, y, de la misma forma, muchas de las fotografías presentadas en 1983 hubieran sido rechazadas diez años antes.

Esta diversidad de opiniones se debe tanto a los cambios ocurridos en modas y actitudes como a los avances tecnológicos en el campo de la fotografía — de nuevo, hay que dejar transcurrir el tiempo antes de definir la naturaleza de dichos cambios. Es evidente que los sucesivos autores de las ediciones del *Photography Yearbook* han utilizado sus propios criterios a la hora de juzgar lo que se podía incluir y lo que no, pero aun teniendo en cuenta los gustos personales de cada uno, si se compara la presente edición con las de 1983 y 1973 veremos claramente que en las dos últimas décadas ha habido varios cambios.

Hay que añadir también que antes de juzgar los cambios en las corrientes fotográficas hay que tener en cuenta los avances en la técnica de ilustración de libros durante estos años, avances que hoy en día permiten ilustrar de forma más fiel los originales monocromos y las fotografías en color.

Quizás el cambio más notable en los últimos veinte años sea la gran popularidad alcanzada por la fotografía en color gracias a su mayor facilidad y al menor coste de las copias en color. Esto, junto con los avances ya mencionados en la técnica de ilustración de libros, se refleja claramente en la composición del *Photography Yearbook*, con su mayor número de páginas en color: 48 en 1973 y 1983 respectivamente, y 112 en esta última edición.

Visualmente, y esto era de esperar, ha habido muchos cambios en el tipo y en el estilo de fotografías presentadas y seleccionadas durante los últimos veinte años. En 1973, muchas de las imágenes en el *Photography Yearbook* buscaban un impacto para dar una impresión fuerte, aunque no del todo satisfactoria; muchos de los retratos — a menudo de personalidades del momento — eran excesivamente grandes y sombríos; había varias fotografías de noticias de actualidad, y las imágenes de ciencias naturales estaban muy por debajo del nivel al que estamos acostumbrados en 1992. Curiosamente, al comparar la sección de datos vemos que hay muy poca diferencia en el tipo de cámaras utilizadas hace veinte años y ahora. Lo que ha cambiado es que el zoom — una más reciente adición al equipo fotográfico — se utiliza ahora con mayor frecuencia.

El *Photography Yearbook* de 1983 da una impresión muy distinta. Diez años más tarde, parece como si los contribuyentes no se tomaran la vida tan en serio ya que hay bastante humor en sus obras. No obstante, algunas de las obras experimentales resultan un tanto artificiales y, de nuevo, las imágenes de paisaje y de ciencias naturales son de menor calidad y menos emotivas que las de hoy. Aunque la edición de 1983 contiene menos fotografías de noticias de actualidad, hay varios retratos de miembros de la familia real y de personas famosas, algunos bastante humorísticos. También hay que notar que el estilo típico de los fotógrafos de Europa de este — expertos en el arte de convertir lo ordinario en algo interesante — hizo una gran contribución a la edición de ese año.

Quizás sea de extrañar que ninguno de los fotógrafos de la edición de 1973, y sólo dos de la de 1983, estén representados este año. También hay que notar que menos de la cuarta parte de las fotografías de la edición de 1973, y menos de la mitad de las de 1983, serían aceptables este año. Obviamente, los avances tecnológicos (así como las modas y gustos personales hasta cierto punto) influyen en esto, pero el factor más importante debe ser el gran aumento experimentado en los últimos años en la calidad de las fotografías presentadas, de manera que el autor de la presente edición tiene para seleccionar un mayor número de obras que sus antecesores.

El carácter internacional del *Photography Yearbook* ha aumentado también en los últimos veinte años, pasando de veintiún países representados en 1973, a treinta y dos en la presente edición. Los profundos transtornos políticos en Europa y la recesión económica mundial no parecen haber afectado el deseo de los fotógrafos contemporáneos de ver sus obras publicadas en el *Photography Yearbook* de 1993 — tenemos más fotografías, y de mayor calidad, este año que en los años anteriores. Quizás sea éste el cambio más importante ocurrido en los últimos veinte años — más y mejores fotografías presentadas, y más y mejores fotografías seleccionadas y publicadas. Y esto sólo puede ser un cambio para el bien.

PETER WILKINSON, FRPS
Editor, Agosto 1992

El plazo para recibir material para su posible inclusión en la próxima edición del Photography Yearbook se cierra el 31 de enero de 1993, y esto se aplicará a los años subsiguientes.

Las transparencias en color pueden ser de cualquier tamaño pero no montadas en vidrio. Si las fotografías en color existen como copia en papel y como transparencia, preferimos la transparencia. Las copias en papel, ya sean en blanco y negro o en color, deberán ir sin borde y tener un mínimo de 18 x 24cm y un máximo de 30 x 40cm. Las copias en papel deberán ir siempre enviadas de forma plana, no enrolladas. Todas las obras presentadas llevarán el nombre del autor y cualquier tipo de información relativa al lugar o sujeto fotografiados, así como cualquier punto de interés relativo a la fotografía, el tipo y marca de cámara, lente y película empleadas.

Si el embalaje es adecuado para su devolución y se cubren los gastos de envío con un cheque en libras esterlinas, giro postal o doce Cupones de Envío Internacional, las obras serán devueltas una vez hecha la selección y terminado el libro. Las participaciones de fuera del Reino Unido serán devueltas por correo ordinario a no ser que se cubran los gastos adicionales de correo aéreo.

Aunque se tomarán las medidas adecuadas, Fountain Press no se hace responsable de ninguna pérdida o daño que pueda sufrir el material. Aunque los derechos de autor sobre las obras seleccionadas seguirán en posesión del mismo, el editor se reserva el derecho a utilizarlas como publicidad del Photography Yearbook.

Los fotógrafos que sean seleccionados recibirán, además del prestigio de ser incluidos en sus páginas, una copia del Photography Yearbook y honorarios por cada reproducción. De ser requerido, y siempre que sea posible, la editorial pondrá en contacto a futuros compradores con los autores de las fotografías seleccionadas.

DAVID TACK

THE ROYAL PHOTOGRAPHIC SOCIETY

JOIN THE POWER BEHIND PHOTOGRAPHY

As a special offer, readers of 'PHOTOGRAPHY YEARBOOK' are being given the opportunity of three months free membership. Join the society now, and receive fifteen months membership for the price of twelve. Write now to the membership officer, THE ROYAL PHOTOGRAPHIC SOCIETY, Milsom Street, Bath BA1 1DN (Telephone 0225 462841 or Fax 0225 448688). Be sure to mark your request 'PYB 1993'.

HIN MUN LEE, FRPS

CHARLES JOB, CARBON PRINT, 1905

Develop the potential of your photography — membership of The Royal Photographic Society is open to everyone, whether you are a total beginner, a dedicated amateur or a full time professional in the imaging world.

An action packed programme of over 250 events a year awaits you — workshops, lectures, masterclasses, conferences, field trips and you would be welcomed at every single event.

Achieve — many who joined as beginners are now Fellows of the Society. Take advantage of the support and encouragement readily available to work towards one of the Society's distinctions. Remember, if you are successful you can use the letters FRPS, ARPS or LRPS after your name.

Enjoy a choice of magazines — The Photographic Journal and the Journal of Photographic Science, both of which come free to every member.

Seize the opportunity to become part of a wide network of fellow photographers so you can meet and learn with some of Britain's most highly recognised practitioners.

Adventure into different areas of photography by joining the experts in 13 specialist groups — Archaeology and Heritage, Audio Visual, Colour, Contemporary, Film & Video, Historical, Holography, Imaging Science and Technology, Medical, Pictorial, Nature, Travel and Visual Journalism.

Explore the work of the earliest photographers in the Society's extensive and world famous collection of rare photographs, books, equipment and periodicals by Fox Talbot, Julia Margaret Cameron, Ansel Adams, Edward Weston, Yousef Karsch, Edward Steichen and many, many more.

Visit the Society's nationally recognised centre of photography in Bath, view at first hand exciting and stimulating work from historical and documentary images to the scientific and very avant garde. Immerse yourself in the comprehensive array of books, posters and postcards in the shop; make yourself at home in the members Club Room, or entertain in the restaurant. Bring a friend — entry is free to members and a guest.

And it doesn't matter where you live — there are 14 regions in Britain each with its own regional organiser and members in over 40 countries abroad, many of which have their own society representative.

THE PHOTOGRAPHERS

THE PHOTOGRAPHERS

THE
PHOTOGRAPHS

Laurie Campbell ■ United Kingdom **17**

B W Mullins ▪ Australia

20 Shelagh Ross ■ United Kingdom

22 George McCarthy ■ United Kingdom

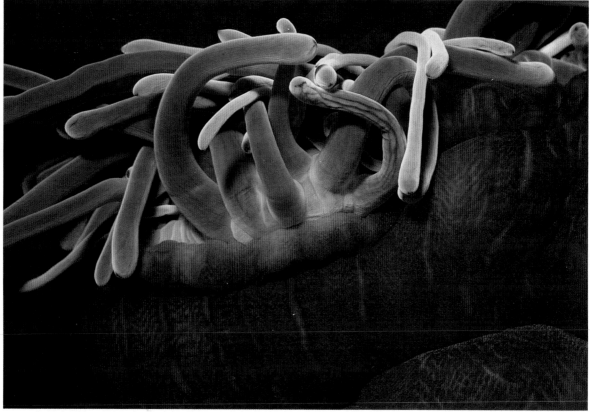

28 W Lawson Wood ▪ United Kingdom

May Van Den Heuvel ■ The Netherlands **39**

Martin Pope ▪ United Kingdom

44 Lloyd Wright ■ United Kingdom

46 Bretislav Marek ■ Czechoslovakia

48 Rudy Lewis ■ United Kingdom

54 Mark Hamblin ■ United Kingdom

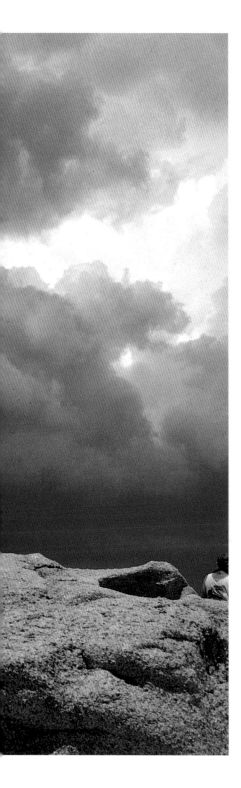

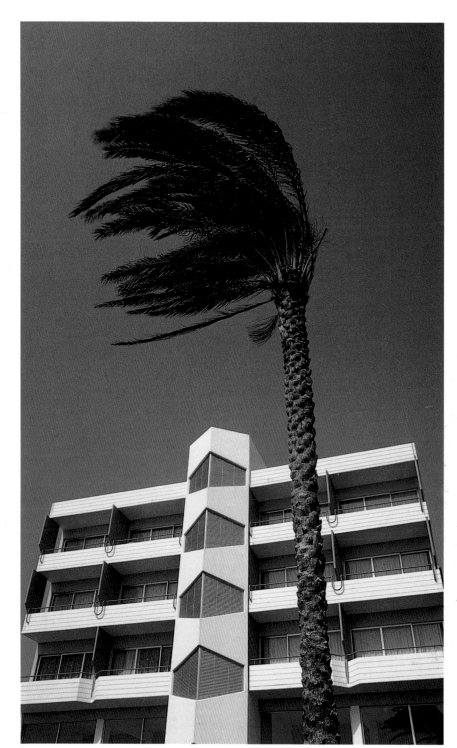

M Kucharski United Kingdom **57**

Tim Rudman ▪ United Kingdom

Peter Gennard ■ United Kingdom

David Cooke ■ United Kingdom **67**

72 J A Wigley ■ United Kingdom

78 Sergei Buslenko ▪ Ukraine

Mark Hamblin ▪ United Kingdom **85**

90 J P Owen ▪ United Kingdom

94 Neeraj Paul ■ India

Sergei Buslenko ▪ Ukraine

S J Parry ▪ United Kingdom

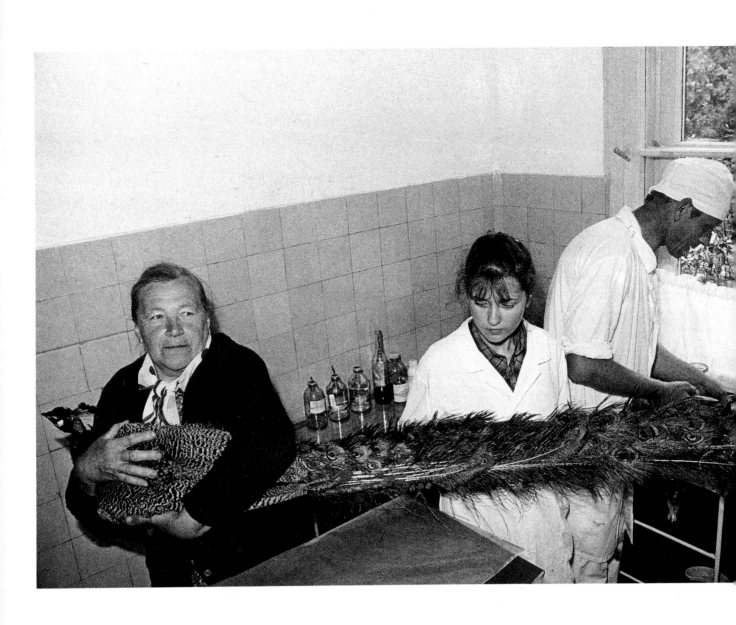

Tim Rudman ▪ United Kingdom

Susan Brown ■ United Kingdom **111**

Anthony Wharton ■ United Kingdom   Paul Mount ■ United Kingdom **117**

120 Samuel Shats ▪ Israel

124 Roy Smith ▪ United Kingdom

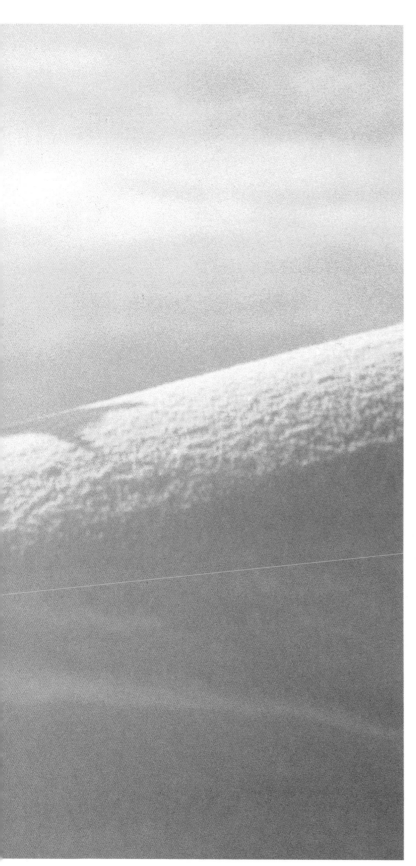

Andrew Gasson ■ United Kingdom **127**

Neil Griffin ■ United Kingdom   David Abiaw ■ United Kingdom **129**

Jan Sobotka ▪ Czechoslovakia

132 Roger Hance ▪ United Kingdom

134 Hugh Milsom ▪ United Kingdom

142 Kevin Broadbery ▪ Denmark

Donald Trott ■ United Kingdom

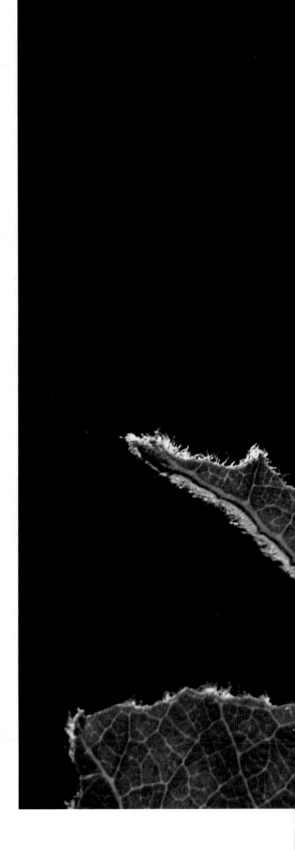

154 Rosemary Calvert ■ Canada

156 Roland Otterstein ■ Canada

Roy Cleaver

158 Jon Thormodsson ▪ Iceland

Malcolm Beaumont ▪ United Kingdom **159**

164 Clint Randall ▪ United Kingdom

172 Peter Hallam ▪ United Kingdom

174 A Baldacchino ■ Malta

Anne Crabbe ■ United Kingdom **175**

176 Hugh Milsom ▪ United Kingdom

M R Szamody ▪ Hungary **177**

178 E A Janes ■ United Kingdom

180 Richard Hayman ▪ United Kingdom

Richard Hayman ● United Kingdom **181**

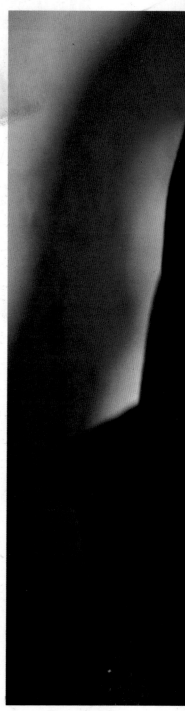

Roger Reynolds United Kingdom **185**

S O Harding ▪ United Kingdom

192 Bela Jansky ▪ United States of America

Peter Brough ■ United Kingdom **197**

198 Ferenc Wagner ■ Hungary

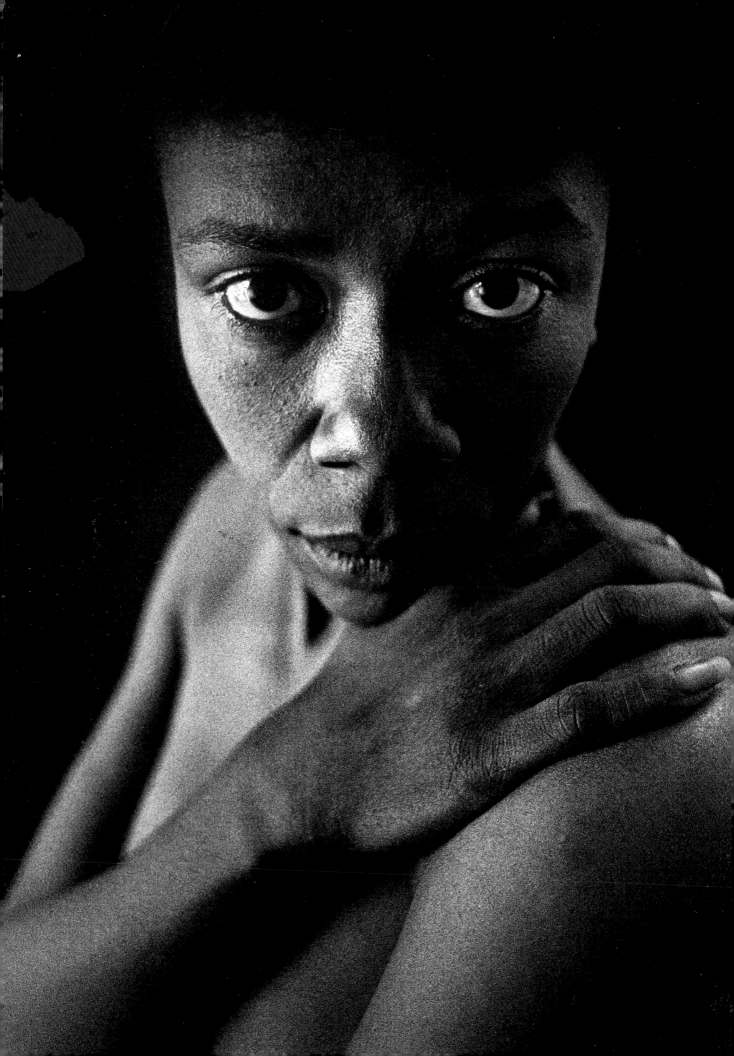

Luis Mikowski ▪ Argentina

Andrew Stark ▪ Australia   Chris Wainwright ▪ United Kingdom **207**

Cliff Thompson ▪ United Kingdom **211**

Francisco Marquez ■ Spain **213**

216 Tony Hamblin ▪ United Kingdom

218 Amit Kr Dan ▪ India

Kenji Nakabayashi ■ Japan **221**

224 C H Burrows ■ United Kingdom

TECHNICAL DATA

PAGE 44

Photographer	Lloyd Wright (UK)
Subject/Location	Garry Glitter in a Slice of Saturday at Liverpool Empire, England
Camera	Nikon F3
Lens	300mm
Film	1/60th at f2.8 on Fuji Neopan 1600

PAGE 45

Photographer	Lloyd Wright (UK)
Subject/Location	David Bowie at the Royal Court, Liverpool, England
Camera	Nikon F3
Lens	180mm
Film	1/60th at f2.8 on Fuji Neopan 1600

PAGE 46/47

Photographer	Bretislav Marek (Czechosolvakia)
Camera	Mamiya R267
Lens	110mm
Film	Orwo

PAGE 48

Photographer	Rudy Lewis (UK)
Subject/Location	Dentist at work in Lhasa, Tibet
Camera	Nikon F2
Lens	85mm
Film	Kodak TRI-X

PAGE 49

Photographer	Jutta Dobler (Germany)
Subject/Location	Souzhen, China
Camera	Nikon

PAGE 50

Photographer	Anthony Wharton (UK)
Subject/Location	The Crooked House, Lavenham, England
Camera	Pentax SFXN
Lens	15mm
Film	Kodachrome

PAGE 51

Photographer	Anthony Wharton (UK)
Subject/Location	Bow Windows, England
Camera	Pentax LX
Lens	15mm
Film	Kodachrome 64

PAGE 52

Photographer	Steven Grueber (USA)
Subject/Location	Yagua Indian Children, Amazon, Eastern Peru
Camera	Canon T90
Lens	80-200mm Zoom
Film	Kodachrome 200

PAGE 53

Photographer	Steven Grueber (USA)
Subject/Location	Yagua Indian Children, Amazon, Eastern Peru
Camera	Canon T90
Lens	80-200mm Zoom
Film	Kodachrome 200

PAGE 54

Photographer	Mark Hamblin (UK)
Subject/Location	Lake Baringo, Kenya
Camera	Canon T90
Lens	500mm Canon
Film	Kodachrome 200

PAGE 55

Photographer	Bill Ivy (Canada)
Subject/Location	Curious Cow Moose, Algonquin Park, Ontario, Canada

PAGE 56

Photographer	Lewis Woodhouse (UK)
Subject/Location	Jeffreys Pine VIII, Yosemite, USA
Camera	Canon EOS 600
Lens	35-135mm Zoom
Film	Kodachrome 64

PAGE 57

Photographer	M. Kucharski (UK)
Subject/Location	Paphos, Cyprus
Camera	Nikon FM
Lens	28mm Nikkor
Film	Kodachrome 64

PAGE 58

Photographer	Pratap Surana (India)
Subject/Location	Open Bill Stork, Ranganathittu Bird Sanctuary, India
Camera	Nikon F-501
Lens	75-250mm Zoom

PAGE 59 (UPPER)

Photographer	Pratap Surana (India)
Subject/Location	Painted Stork, Kokkre Bellur, India
Camera	Nikon F-501
Lens	75-250mm Tamron

PAGE 59 (LOWER)

Photographer	Pratap Surana (India)
Subject/Location	Spoon Bill, Ranganathittu Bird Sanctuary, India
Camera	Nikon F-501
Lens	75-150mm Zoom

PAGE 60

Photographer	Tim Rudman (UK)
Subject/Location	Tadley, Hampshire, England
Camera	Ricoh KR 10 Super
Lens	50mm
Film	Fujichrome RD 100

PAGE 61

Photographer	E. A. Janes (UK)
Subject/Location	Ullswater, Cumberland, England
Camera	Hasselblad CM
Lens	50mm Distagon Wide Angle
Film	Ektachrome 120

PAGE 62

Photographer	Joerg Hoffman (Germany)
Subject/Location	Dusseldorf, Germany
Camera	Nikon F3
Lens	35mm
Film	Fujichrome 100

PAGE 63

Photographer	Joerg Hoffmann (Germany)
Subject/Location	Cologne, Germany
Camera	Nikon F801s
Lens	24mm
Film	Fujichrome 100

PAGE 64

Photographer	Brian Randle (UK)
Subject/Location	Cruft Dog Show 1992, Birmingham National Exhibition Centre, England
Camera	Canon EOS 1
Lens	35-70mm Canon EF Zoom
Film	Fujicolor Super HG 400

PAGE 65 (UPPER & LOWER)

Photographer	Peter Gennard (UK)
Subject/Location	Cruft Dog Show 1992, Birmingham National Exhibition Centre, England
Camera	Nikon FE
Lens	85mm Nikkor
Film	Fuji Neopan 400

PAGE 66

Photographer	Rhonda Milner (Australia)
Camera	Nikon FM2
Lens	50mm
Film	Ilford HP5

PAGE 67

Photographer	David Cooke (UK)
Camera	Nikon FM2
Film	Kodak TR1-X

PAGE 68

Photographer	Tony Worobiec (UK)
Subject/Location	'Garys Hotrod', Exeter, England
Camera	Mamiya 645s
Lens	35mm
Film	1/15th at f16 on Ilford FP4

PAGE 69

Photographer	Tony Worobiec (UK)
Subject/Location	'Silver Machine', Wincanton, England
Camera	Mamiya 645s
Lens	35mm
Film	1/60th at f16 on Ilford FP4

PAGE 70

Photographer	G. L. Morgans (UK)
Subject/Location	Neath Valley, South Wales
Camera	Minolta X300
Lens	35-70mm Minolta Zoom
Film	Ilford XP2

PAGE 71

Photographer	G. L. Morgans (UK)
Subject/Location	Pit Ponies, Neath Valley, South Wales
Camera	Minolta X300
Lens	35-70mm Minolta Zoom
Film	Ilford XP2

PAGE 166

Photographer	Vaclav Lahovsky (Czechoslovakia)
Subject/Location	Pavza, Czechoslovakia
Camera	Kiev
Lens	300mm
Film	Orwo NP22

PAGE 167

Photographer	Graham Burstow (Australia)
Subject/Location	Beach Beauty Contest, Gold Coast, Australia
Camera	Pentax ES
Lens	28mm Takumar
Film	Kodak T-Max 400

PAGE 168-169

Photographer	Arnold Hubbard (UK)
Subject/Location	Weardale, Co. Durham, England
Camera	Mamiyaflex C220
Lens	80mm Sekor
Film	Ilford FP4

PAGE 170

Photographer	Helene Rogers (UK)
Subject/Location	Portrait of Jaroslav Novotny, A top Czechoslovakian photographer
Camera	Canon F1
Lens	24mm
Film	Ilford XP1

PAGE 171

Photographer	T. Narayan (India)

PAGE 172

Photographer	Peter Hallam (UK)
Subject/Location	Wreck of the Helvetia, Rossilli, South Wales
Camera	Olympus OM1N
Lens	24mm
Film	Ilford FP4

PAGE 173

Photographer	M. R. Owaisi (Pakistan)
Subject/Location	Dawn at the River Jhelum, Pakistan
Camera	Pentax 6 x 7
Lens	35mm Pentax Fish Eye
Film	Forte

PAGE 174

Photographer	A. Baldacchino (Malta)
Camera	Mamiya
Lens	250mm
Film	Kodak T-Max

PAGE 175

Photographer	Anne Crabbe (UK)
Subject/Location	Mother & Daughter
Camera	Hasselblad
Lens	80mm
Film	Ilford HP5

PAGE 176

Photographer	Hugh Milsom (UK)
Subject/Location	Reeds, Snape, Suffolk, England
Camera	Canon A1
Lens	24mm Tokina
Film	Kodak Technical Pan

PAGE 177

Photographer	M. R. Szamody (Hungary)

PAGE 178

Photographer	E. A. Janes (UK)
Subject/Location	Infant Chimpanzee, Whipsnade Wild Animal Park, Bedford, England
Camera	Hasselblad CM
Lens	150mm Sonar
Film	Fujichrome 50

PAGE 179

Photographer	E. A. Janes (UK)
Subject/Location	Orang-utan and infant, Twycross Zoo, England
Camera	Canon T90
Lens	100-300mm Zoom
Film	Kodachrome 64

PAGE 180

Photographer	Richard Hayman (UK)
Subject/Location	Tower Bridge, London, England
Camera	Nikon FE
Lens	28mm – Moon added with 75-150mm Zoom
Film	Fujichrome Velvia

PAGE 181

Photographer	Richard Hayman (UK)
Subject/Location	Houses of Parliament, London
Camera	Nikon FM2
Lens	50mm-1/20th at f8
Film	Fujichrome Velvia

PAGE 182

Photographer	Pranlal Patel (India)
Subject/Location	Kutch, Gujarat, India
Camera	Nikon FM2
Lens	50mm
Film	Fujichrome

PAGE 183

Photographer	Van Greaves (UK)
Subject/Location	Eastern Cyprus
Camera	Nikon F-801
Lens	75-300mm Sigma Zoom
Film	Fujichrome 100

PAGE 184

Photographer	Roger Reynolds (UK)
Subject/Location	Hardanger Fjord, Norway
Camera	Mamya 645
Lens	24mm
Film	Fujicolour Professional 100

PAGE 185

Photographer	Roger Reynolds (UK)
Subject/Location	Storm at Eidfjord, Norway
Camera	Mamya 645
Lens	24mm
Film	Fujicolor Professional 100

PAGE 186

Photographer	Ines Roberts (USA)
Subject/Location	Gypsy in Cracow, Poland
Camera	Minolta XD5

PAGE 187

Photographer	Ines Roberts (USA)
Subject/Location	Cracow, Poland
Camera	Minolta XD5

PAGE 188

Photographer	David Nicholls (Canada)
Subject/Location	Bryce Canyon, Utah, USA
Camera	Nikon F4
Lens	80-200mm Nikkor Zoom
Film	Kodachrome 64

PAGE 189

Photographer	David Nicholls (Canada)
Subject/Location	Saguaro Forest, Arizona, USA
Camera	Nikon F4
Lens	80-200mm Nikkor Zoom
Film	Kodachrome 64

PAGE 190

Photographer	S. O. Harding (UK)
Subject/Location	Colour of Europe Festival, Festival Hall, London
Camera	Nikon FA
Lens	75-150mm Nikkor Zoom
Film	Fuji 100

PAGE 191

Photographer	S. O. Harding (UK)
Subject/Location	Notting Hill Carnival, London
Camera	Nikon FA
Lens	75-105 Nikkor Zoom
Film	Orwo 50

PAGE 192

Photographer	Bela Janszky (USA)
Subject/Location	Maharaja's Palace, Jaipur, India
Camera	Canon Ftb
Lens	135mm Canon
Film	Eastman Kodak

PAGE 193

Photographer	Victor Attfield (UK)
Subject/Location	Positano, Italy
Camera	Nikkormat FT3
Lens	28mm Nikkor

PAGE 194

Photographer	Ivan Cisar (Czechoslovakia)
Subject/Location	Prague, Czechoslovakia
Camera	Pentax Super
Lens	28-80mm Zoom
Film	Orwo NP22

PAGE 195

Photographer	Fernando Casanueva (Argentina)
Camera	Nikon F3
Lens	28mm
Film	Ilford HP5 Plus

PAGE 196-197

Photographer	Peter Brough (UK)
Subject/Location	Wheelchair Games, St Helens, Lancs, England
Camera	Canon A1
Lens	80-200mm Zoom
Film	Kodak T-Max

PAGE 198

Photographer	Ferenc Wagner (Hungary)
Camera	Canon A1
Lens	50mm
Film	Orwo NP22

PAGE 199

Photographer	Laszlo Dobosy (Hungary)
Camera	Minolta X700
Lens	16mm Rokkor
Film	Orwo NP20

PAGE 200

Photographer	Rudy Lewis (UK)
Subject/Location	Peking, China
Camera	Nikon F2
Lens	85mm
Film	Kodak TR1-X

PAGE 201

Photographer	Rudy Lewis (UK)
Subject/Location	Kathmandu, Nepal
Camera	Nikon F2A
Lens	28mm Nikkor
Film	Kodak TR1-X

PAGE 202

Photographer	Romualdas Pozerskis (Lithuania)
Camera	Minolta X700
Lens	24mm
Film	Suema 80

PAGE 203

Photographer	E. Emyrus Jones (UK)
Subject/Location	Open Air Market, Oldham, Lancashire, England
Camera	Mamyaflex
Lens	80mm
Film	Ilford FP4

PAGE 204

Photographer	Luis Mikowski (Argentina)
Camera	Canon T90
Lens	20mm
Film	Kodak TR1-X

PAGE 205

Photographer	Tony Butcher (UK)
Camera	Canon T90
Lens	90mm Tamron
Film	Ilford FP4

PAGE 206

Photographer	Andrew Stark (Australia)
Subject/Location	Surry Hills, Sydney, Australia
Camera	Konica TC
Lens	40mm
Film	Kodak TR1-X

PAGE 207

Photographer	Chris Wainwright (UK)
Subject/Location	Wedding at Bray, England
Camera	Canon AE1
Lens	135mm
Film	Ilford FP4

PAGE 208

Photographer	Tim Rudman (UK)
Subject/Location	Surrey, England
Camera	Yashica TL Electro
Lens	24mm
Film	Ilford FP4

PAGE 209

Photographer	Pam Gaston (UK)
Subject/Location	Berkeley, Gloucestershire, England
Camera	Nikon FM2
Lens	50mm
Film	Fujichrome 100

PAGE 210

Photographer	D. D. Mullins (Australia)
Subject/Location	'Miners Return', Scotland
Camera	Nikon FA
Film	Kodachrome 64

PAGE 211

Photographer	Cliff Thompson (UK)
Subject/Location	A posterisation employing two slides as original sources, both taken near Jaiselmer, North India. Desert background was taken on a Canon EOS 600 with 50mm lens. The camel was taken on the same camera using 100-300mm zoom lens. The final posterised image was taken using an Olympus OM2N fitted with a 90mm Tokina macro lens
Film	Kodak Ektachrome 64

PAGE 212

Photographer	F. Forleo (South Africa)
Camera	Olympus OM4
Lens	500mm
Film	Fuji

PAGE 213

Photographer	Francisco Marquez (Spain)
Subject/Location	Greater Flamingo, "Fuente de Piedra" Wetland, Malaga, Spain
Camera	Nikon F4s
Lens	105mm Nikkor
Film	Kodachrome 200 Professional

PAGE 214-215

Photographer	Leo Dosremedios (USA)
Subject/Location	Bend, Oregon, USA
Camera	Nikon 8008
Lens	70-210mm
Film	Kodachrome 200

PAGE 216

Photographer	Tony Hamblin (UK)
Subject/Location	Spiny Softshell Turtle, Everglades, Florida, USA
Camera	Canon T90
Lens	500mm
Film	Kodachrome 64

PAGE 217

Photographer	Eric Bird (UK)
Subject/Location	Giant Tortoises, Island of Santa Cruz, Galapagos, Ecuador
Camera	Nikon F4s
Lens	500mm Nikkor
Film	Kodachrome 200

PAGE 218

Photographer	Amit Kr Dan (India)
Subject/Location	Perulia, India
Camera	Olympus OM1
Lens	135mm
Film	Fujichrome 100

PAGE 219

Photographer	Amit Kr Dan (India)
Subject/Location	Perulia, India
Camera	Olympus OM1
Lens	50mm
Film	Fujichrome 100

PAGE 220

Photographer	Kenji Nakabayashi (Japan)
Subject/Location	Lake Tanuki, near Mount Fuji, Japan
Camera	Hasselblad 500cm
Lens	Distagon 4/50
Film	Ektachrome 64

PAGE 221

Photographer	Kenji Nakabayashi (Japan)
Subject/Location	Fuji City, Japan
Camera	Nikon F4
Lens	75-300mm AF Nikkor Zoom
Film	Ektachrome 64

PAGE 222

Photographer	Manfred Hermann (Germany)
Subject/Location	Germany
Camera	Nikon F-601
Lens	28-70mm Sigma Zoom
Film	Fujichrome 100

PAGE 223

Photographer	Jonathan Plant (UK)
Subject/Location	Green Frog, Ontario, Canada
Camera	Canon AE1P
Lens	135mm with extension tube and flash
Film	Fujichrome Velvia

PAGE 224

Photographer	C. H. Burrows (UK)
Subject/Location	Campolongo Pass, Corvara, Italy
Camera	Leica M2
Lens	50mm
Film	Kodachrome

BACK ENDPAPER

Photographer	Raymond Young (UK)
Subject/Location	The Tamar Bridges, Plymouth, Devon, England
Camera	Pentax SP500
Lens	55mm Takumar
Film	Ilford PAN F